Teaching Large Classes

Allan J. Gedalof

London, Canada

STLHE SAPES Society for Teaching and Learning in Higher Education

La société pour l'avancement de la pédagogie dans l'enseignement supérieur

STLHE Green Guides

Series Editors:

W. Alan Wright
Université du Québec
UQAR: Campus de Lévis
Lévis, QC G6V 8R9

Eileen Herteis
Purdy Crawford Teaching Centre
Mount Allison University
Sackville, NB E4L 1B7

Christopher Knapper
Instructional Development Centre
Queen's University,
Kingston, ON K7L 3N6

Carol O'Neil
Centre for Learning and Teaching
Dalhousie University
Halifax, NS B3H 4J3

Publishing Co-ordinator: Debra Dawson,
Teaching Support Centre,
The University of Western Ontario

Director of Retail Services: Steve Alb, The Book Store at Western
The University of Western Ontario

© Society for Teaching and Learning in Higher Education, 2004
Ninth printing, July 2016

Distributed on behalf of STLHE by:

The Book Store at Western,
University Community Centre,
The University of Western Ontario,
London, Ontario N6A 3K7

Canadian Cataloguing in Publication Data
Gedalof, Allan J.
    Teaching large classes
(Green guide series)
Includes bibliographical references
ISBN 0-7703-8464-1

1. College teaching. I. Society for Teaching and Learning in Higher Education. II. Dalhousie University. Office of Instructional Development and Technology. III. Title. IV. Series.

LB2331.G44 1998378.1'25 C98-950129-9

Foreword

With this splendid monograph by Allan Gedalof the Society for Teaching and Learning in Higher Education launches its new series of Green Guides. Each guide will deal with some aspect of teaching and learning in higher education. They will be solidly based on relevant research and theory, but the approach will be pragmatic and applied. The guides will be short, with an emphasis on clear, jargon-free expression, and plentiful examples of how the ideas being discussed relate to real teaching situations faced by Canadian academics. Another feature of the guides is their reasonable price, which is made possible by the generous donation of time by STLHE members in writing, reviewing, editing, and distributing these valuable resources.

The idea of Green Guides originated with our sister organization on the other side of the world, the Higher Education and Research Development Society of Australasia. HERDSA published its first guide in 1984, and they have now published more than 20 guides on a wide range of topics related to teaching and learning in higher education. HERDSA has very generously allowed us to use their title for the series, and we will shortly be embarking on a collaborative endeavour to jointly publish some titles in both Canada and Australia. This arrangement has been greatly facilitated by the generous help of Dr. Kym Fraser of Monash University, who chairs the HERDSA publications committee.

Other Green Guides are in the works and will be published shortly. Meanwhile, any readers inspired to make their own proposals for a new guide are invited to contact one of the series editors.

Christopher Knapper
Alan Wright
Series Editors

Allan J. Gedalof

After earning degrees at Memorial University of Newfoundland, the University of Alberta, and Birkbeck College (University of London), has since 1972 tried his best to teach English Literature, Film, and Popular Culture at the University of Western Ontario. He has won OCUFA (1990) and 3M/STLHE (1991) teaching awards, and made many presentations on aspects of university pedagogy.

Contents

Acknowledgements 8

Preface 9

Preliminary Matters 11

What is a large class? Do you teach one? 11

Some fundamental and general problems 11

Facing our anxiety 12

Passion, intensity, and energy 13

Motivating and modelling 13

Problems of scale 15

Preparing For Large Classes 17

Check out the classroom 17

Talk nicely to the technical support people 17

Think about how to use the room 17

Prepare, prepare, and over-prepare 18

Organization must be seen to be done 18

Have extra material 18

You can only teach two or three big ideas 18

Handouts and bulletin boards 18

Plan your interactive exercises, including questions 20

Make sure everything works before class 20

Be prepared for when technology fails you 20

You need a budget to acquire instructional materials 21

Every problem comes up every year 21

Delivering The Lecture 23

Classroom strategies and behaviours 23

Energy, passion, and intensity 23

Setting the tone, starting the class, ground rules 24

Mobility and body language 25

Physical facts 26

Teach through the senses 26

Repetition and variation 27

Variety in instructional method 28

Eye contact 28

Reading the class 29

Humour works 29

Performing your material 30

Self-revelation 30

Ending the class 30

Starting and finishing on time 31

Erasing your board, tidying your junk 31

Interactive methods: General practices and strategies 31

Begin as you mean to go on 31

Asking questions 32

Responding to questions and comments 33

Using students' personalities 34

Fostering a community of learners 34

Ombuddies 34

Question and suggestion boxes 35

Difficult students 35

Interactive methods for large classes 36

Gathering responses in a batch 36

Brainstorming 36

Quescussion 37

The one-minute paper 38

Large group role playing or mass debate 39

Independent discussion groups 40

Team teaching 41

The tag team 41

The specialists 41

The dance: You lead, I'll follow 42

The rehearsed improvisation 42

The debate and panel discussion 42

The animator and recorder 42

The high wire act 43

Outside The Lecture Hall 45

Tutorials and teaching assistants 45

The make-up of tutorials 45

Working with teaching assistants and tutorial leaders 46

Weekly course meetings 46

Support for Tas 48

Evaluation 49

Teaching aids and technology: The well-equipped classroom 50

A few parting but not final words 52

References 53

Suggestions for further reading 53

About STLHE 55

Acknowledgements

The ideas and suggestions in this handbook could not have been developed without the examples and help of many individuals. In particular, I want to start by thanking those colleagues with whom I have taught and discussed large classes, and from whom I have learned a great deal, especially (in no particular order) Douglas Kneale, Alan Somerset, Manina Jones, Tom Carmichael, Mike Atkinson, Paul Gaudet, Colin Baird, Michael Moore, Alan Blizzard, and Alison Lee. Their examples and precepts inform every part of this work. I also want to thank the legion of underpaid and overworked teaching assistants I have been fortunate to work with and to whom I attribute a great deal of whatever success I may have had in teaching large classes.

Two people have been instrumental in getting this project underway and seeing it to fruition. The energy and commitment of Christopher Knapper (Queen's University) in launching this publication series, taking on the job of general editor, and encouraging me to prepare this guide have been inspirational. Dale Roy of McMaster University has made invaluable comments and suggestions and, for all its faults, this guide would have been even more inadequate without his generous help. These two, along with series co-editor Alan Wright of Dalhousie University, in no small way explain why STLHE is such a valuable and supportive organization for college and university teachers. I would like to give special thanks to my department chair at the University of Western Ontario, Prof. Paul Gaudet, for his support and encouragement and for understanding that publishing broadly on pedagogy is as valuable as working more narrowly within one's special field.

Finally, I want to thank those people who inestimably enrich my life and regularly remind me in all sorts of ways of why sharing what we know and feel is the most rewarding of experiences: my students, my sons Ze'ev and Eli, and my partner in life and teaching, Monique Mailloux.

Preface

In the face of growing programs and shrinking funds, more of us are having to teach large classes for two main reasons. First, to accommodate, with a stable or shrinking complement of faculty members, the burgeoning number of students who deserve to be in university; and second, as a way to preserve smaller classes in some other parts of our programs. Not to put too fine a point upon it, larger class size is a problem and should always and everywhere be resisted. We cannot forget, nor can we let those who have put us in this situation forget, that creating large classes is fundamentally contrary to what university teaching is supposed to do: foster the growth of *individuals*, and encourage them in their individuality so that they become independent, creative, self-motivated, critical thinkers and learners. But given that in the current situation we are obligated to accept the students who deserve to be here, and that we have to teach some large classes as a way to keep other ones small, we might as well do the best job we can of it.

Part of the problem is that we are so ill-prepared for this task in every way. Far too often we lack the individual and institutional will and the technical and staff support to do this job well. It is a bitter irony that at the highest level of education we have the least amount of teacher training. In addition, many faculty have earned their current jobs and past successes by developing skills that often seem to be counter-indicative of good teaching, especially at introductory levels where larger classes seem to be most vigorously proliferating. We prepare for a profession, a large part of which is very public, by doing things that are intensely private, often idiosyncratic. Given this, it is no surprise that most of us come to the profession having experienced predominantly negative examples of how to teach, and many simply accept this as the way university teaching is carried out and valued.

I leave this topic with a familiar anecdote that corroborates the low esteem typically placed on teaching in the academy. It is provided by colleagues in all disciplines who, in an annual exercise of vernal thanksgiving on campuses across the country, repeat the formula "Thank God the students are gone. Now I can get on with my *real* work." Well, if you take on teaching large classes, that will become a huge part of your real work. You may have to labour hard to get your colleagues to understand and recognize the contribution you are making to your department, discipline, and institution, and to give your course the equipment, resources, and staff you will need to make it work well.

Despite these reservations about teaching large classes, I should acknowledge that I feel differently on good days, when I have the right resources and have done the preparation required to use them in a manner commensurate with the size of the class, and things have gone really well, both students and instructors can experience a buzz, a rush that comes from having shared an exciting common experience. And that excitement can go beyond that generated by small classes: scale can affect a class and its members both positively and negatively.

Two caveats regarding how to take and use what follows

Everything that follows is to be understood as a series of suggestions rather than an attempt to be definitive, prescriptive or normative, and no one will want or be able to do all of the things described or discussed. While I have tried in what follows to set out strategies, techniques, policies, and practices that will be as widely adoptable and adaptable as possible, in the end part of our value as teachers is that we do the job in unique ways. In large classes, where performance takes on greater importance than in smaller classes, individual personality and style figure very prominently indeed: I teach the way I teach because I am who I am, teaching what I teach. Nevertheless, many basic things are transferable and broadly desirable, and I have tried to focus on those and to offer a range of suggestions when I go beyond them. While what follows is written with the novice teacher of large classes in mind, I hope that experienced teachers will find things of use to them also.

The second caveat concerns the **content and structure** of lectures for large classes. These are subjects I will not discuss at any great length in this handbook. For the most part, sound practice in these aspects of lecture preparation is the same for large and small classes: solid content, clear and apparent organization and signposts, lucid thinking, are hallmarks of good teaching regardless of class size, and there are many places that the inquiring university teacher can turn to for help with basic lecturing techniques and strategies. Here, I will only discuss issues of content and organization where they are at least in part driven by the particular circumstances of working in large classes.

Preliminary Matters

What is a large class anyway? Do you teach one?

That first question is not an easy one to answer, nor do I believe that the magic number, the great divide between large and less-than-large, is fixed or constant. Despite that belief, it is interesting to note that the threshold number most frequently quoted in the growing body of studies on teaching large classes is the same as the one I arrived at on the basis of my less-than-scientific and idiosyncratic measure. A large class is one in which I cannot make individual, protracted eye contact with each student in the room over the course of a standard 50-minute period. Behind this measure stands my view that I am not teaching a collective entity but a number of individuals, each of whom responds differently to the material under discussion and to my approach to it. In order to gauge students' involvement in the class and comprehension of material, I need to monitor them very carefully. In a 50-minute class I can engage or make a connection with about one student per minute, so for me a large class is more than 50 individuals.

There are two other measures, also floating and individual, that are factored into this. The first is purely practical, and relates simply to the numbers of hours in a day and days in a school year. Time places constraints on the number of students for whom I can do all of the marking, and make careful and extensive comments on essays and other assignments. The second factor is perhaps a function of my mental capacity, but more probably is a psychological barrier (there is a study here for someone else to do): it is the number of names I feel comfortable in learning. In my experience, I seem to be daunted by the prospect of learning the names of members of a group of more than about 50.

Another hypothetical number to keep in mind here is the one that marks the point at which large classes become *very* large classes and teaching strategies have to be modified even further. In my experience, this happens when class sizes go over 400, and I will make specific suggestions for such classes when appropriate.

Some fundamental and general problems in teaching large classes

Both teachers and students in large classes face a number of physical and psychological problems that have to be confronted. For professors, it is not enough to just talk louder, write bigger, and make larger gestures, although sometimes those things help. Perhaps more telling than the physical problems of being heard and seen, of finding ways to deliver material clearly and forcefully to a large group, are the difficulties of overcoming the psychological effects we and the students feel as part of a potentially faceless, undifferentiated mass. It is worth bearing in mind that if the faces of the students further back in the room are nothing but a blur to you, that is probably how you appear to them too. And if you are anxious about speaking to students, how might they feel about speaking up in class?

Facing our anxiety

One of the first problems in confronting this blur probably precedes entry to the classroom, and that concerns our own nervousness. I face all first classes, regardless of size, with a degree of trepidation, and the degree rises in direct proportion to class size. I have long thought of first meetings with classes as being very like first dates, with all the usual tormenting doubts. Will they like me? Will they find me interesting? Will there be some kind of chemistry among us? Do I provide something they want and need? Will I like them? Do we have anything to say to each other? Will we want to see each other again? That I feel this way, have these anxieties, I once regarded as a problem or inadequacy, which of course made me feel even more inadequate. This attitude persisted until I team-taught a first-year course, enrolment 125, with an 18-years-my-senior colleague in my department, and incidentally the individual I most respected as a teacher.

I arrived a few minutes early for the class, stomach a-flutter, anxious not only with my usual first-class worries but also because I was teaching with someone whose judgement I respect and care about, to find my colleague already there. I sat down beside him, exchanged the usual salutations, and then noticed his white-knuckled grasp of his lecture notes. "You're not nervous, are you?" I asked. Indeed he was, he explained, at the beginning of every course, and to a lesser extent at the beginning of every lecture. Once his state of nerves had, as it were, sanctioned mine, I understood that part of what had made my colleague such a formidable teacher was that he continued to care passionately about teaching well and effectively throughout his career. His performance anxiety did not hinder his teaching but helped to raise his level of intensity and energy. There is no doubt that intensity and energy, coupled with his passion for his subject (and, not incidentally, his extraordinary knowledge, fierce intellect, and high expectations and demands of himself and his students) were in large measure responsible for his success as a teacher.

Knowing that others are as nervous as we are offers some comfort, but can hardly eliminate nervousness on its own. Other things that might help include the following:

- If you have the opportunity, try your presentation out on smaller, even informal groups first, working up to larger groups in larger classes. Talking to a small group in a large lecture theatre, or trying parts of your lecture out, with the accompanying technology, in an empty large classroom, can help you get used to the dynamics and demands of the room.
- Every large class will have students who take it upon themselves to radiate approval. They smile or nod their heads when you look at them. In early classes you may find it encouraging to discover those students (they usually sit near the front) and focus on them rather than on the class at large.

- Visit large classes taught by successful teachers in your department or faculty. See how they do it, and pick their brains.

Passion, intensity, and energy

Among the list of qualities that would distinguish any teacher, regardless of class size, I want to draw particular attention to the closely related traits of passion, intensity, and energy. While these may manifest themselves in different teachers in a great number of ways, I believe them to be the *sine qua non* of superior teaching. The best teachers I know, regardless of discipline, consistently display a passion for their subjects, and the willingness to put that passion on display in the classroom informs and fires their teaching and plays a major role in their successes. During a group discussion of this very subject among teaching award winners, one of my quietest, least histrionic or demonstrative colleagues looked down at the table rather than directly at those sitting around it, and confessed to passion in the workplace. "Something," he said, "happens to me when I step into the classroom." And it should happen to all of us. I do not mean that we all have to become whirling dervishes sparking high-octane ideas at every turn, or that starting blocks should be installed outside every classroom door. We each have a range of classroom behaviours available and appropriate to us, and passion, intensity, and energy can be expressed in a controlled and quiet way just as well as they can be communicated loudly and emotionally. The important thing is that we feel and in some way demonstrate passion for our subjects and care deeply about how we represent them to our students.

Motivating and modelling

The idea of representing or modelling a subject assumes even greater than usual importance when teaching large classes. We can and often do play many different roles as teachers, and the hierarchy of these roles varies from one teacher to another. But prime among them are our tasks of conveying information, teaching skills and concepts, motivating students, and modelling how we practise and engage with our disciplines. What I am arguing here is that, for a variety of reasons, the motivating and modelling functions assume greater importance in larger classes. Here, for instance, is what Habeshaw, Gibbs, and Habeshaw (1993, p. 27) have to say in *53 problems with large classes: Making the best of a bad job:*

> Courses which were designed for a target group of a particular size are not going to be appropriate for a much larger group, where there is less time available, less support for students and where communication is more difficult. As your student numbers increase, you and your colleagues will probably find that it becomes unrealistic to try to meet your former course objectives. ... What is then needed, upsetting though this may be, is a severe pruning of your expectations so that you can concentrate on the really important aspects of your course.

Richard Weaver and Howard Cotrell (1987, p. 67) point to what those "really important aspects of your course" might be when they paint their "ideal picture of lecturers with large audiences," namely:

People in front of audiences who are both sensitive and responsive to the enthusiastic synergy and excitement in their listeners. They provide listeners with means for launching themselves on new adventures in learning, alternatives for moving themselves off dead center when they have reached learning plateaus, and opportunities for overcoming the war weariness that is frequently occasioned in the battle for learning.

Putting aside rhetoric and images even more fulsome than my own, for Weaver and Cotrell, as for many others writing on this subject, the qualities that make a lecturer "ideal" are associated with the ability to motivate, inspire, and relate sympathetically to their students. Such teachers are less concerned with imparting raw content and more with helping students to learn, to *want* to learn, and to learn *how* to learn.

My own experience has confirmed popular wisdom on this subject: in large classes, a teacher must sometimes jettison or streamline part of the course material in order to teach some other parts of it effectively. One reason for this is the very nature of large classes and the phenomena that have given rise to them. Current large first-year classes, for instance, include students with more varied educational, social, ethnic, and cultural backgrounds than was the case in the past — which seems to me a generally good thing. When there is a much greater variety in students' abilities, interests, experiences, and reasons for studying, teachers need to provide more varied examples, more careful explanations, and even repeat things more often. They may also have to spend more time on motivational aspects of teaching. And in large classes, it seems to be more crucial that we provide something beyond mere transmission of information.

The fundamental principle here is this: if nobody is learning, you are just talking, not teaching. Anybody can provide students with facts or with the body of knowledge that comprises a discipline. This can be done with textbooks, articles, handouts, self-instructional programs and packages, audio and videotapes, lecture notes on reserve in the library, printed course notes sold as a package or available on computer disks. Any of these might do the job of merely communicating facts more efficiently than a lecturer reading her or his lecture notes to a group of students frantically scribbling hieroglyphics they will later have profound difficulty in interpreting. Often this seems to be a process whereby a disturbingly mutated version of the professor's notes turns into a student's notes, often without passing through the mind of either. A good teacher, then, will teach primarily not to provide good notes or a body of facts that comprise part of a discipline, but will motivate and teach how to learn, and especially how to learn things that no one has yet taught.

Motivating students to learn, and helping them learn how to learn are paramount goals, ones significantly furthered by displaying passion and enthusiasm for your subject, interest in and sympathy for your students, and energy in your teaching style. But we still have concepts to explain and exemplify, the body of stuff that comprises a subject, field, or discipline to teach.

Problems of scale

Two distinct problems of scale typically occur in large classes, one affecting the behaviour or attitude of professors, and the second course content. One way I try to combat the first of these problems is by characterizing teaching large classes as *Loaves and fishes* or *Trying to make a little professor go a long way.* This messianic allusion is ironic and meant to act as a warning to me and to any professor who believes that because she or he is now addressing the multitudes, there must be something superhuman or divine about this academic mission. This is dangerous thinking. Big classes often give professors an inordinate sense of power and authority, both in their own minds and in those of their students. In part this stems from the fact that we usually appear larger than life in such classes, which seems quite natural under the circumstances. But we might also be less likely to confess to ignorance before so many people, be more likely to believe that because we represent our discipline to such a crowd we had better demonstrate real mastery of that discipline. Obviously, such attitudes get in the way of students developing authority of their own, and falsify our own natures and status as academics. Later on I will discuss how these specific tendencies manifest themselves, and offer some suggestions about countering them.

Very closely related to this point is the principle, easy to lose sight of in large classes, that *it is important to go over the small things, the fundamental building blocks of our disciplines.* I have often found that the definitions of crucial concepts or phenomena that students bring to university are inadequate in one or more ways. They might be largely forgotten or never learned in the first place, unclear, or not sophisticated or complex enough for university use. In my own field, for instance, it would be reckless for me to assume that my students understand the *literary* definitions of terms like "novel" or "irony" even though they might have heard and used those expressions hundreds of times. Often, however, we are affected by constraints of time and scale, and are reluctant to take valuable minutes to explain things that we think everyone should know, or that the majority of students might even believe they know. To a greater or lesser degree, I believe that we all suffer from the syndrome that prompted a frustrated professor to complain to his class that he had been teaching them the same idea for the past 20 years and they still did not know it! Indeed, some things are so fundamental to an understanding or knowledge of our subjects that we grow weary of repeating them, believe that because they are so contemptibly familiar to us they must be known by all.

Richard Goranson (1976) addresses exactly this issue in his very useful article, *A paradox in educational communication.* He demonstrates that (p. 65) "after the solution to a problem is known, the problem itself appears to be inherently less difficult" and the difficulty of a lot of the material we teach is characteristically and severely underestimated by those who have already worked it through. Do not be afraid then to say the obvious, take baby steps, or to repeat to yourself the formula I use to guard against contempt, born of familiarity, for basic knowledge: "It is all news to them," I regularly tell myself and my teaching assistants.

Some strategies that might help in correctly estimating the difficulty of material are:

- looking at students' notes after class to see what they have or have not grasped;
- checking for clarity by asking appropriate questions after a unit has been covered;
- giving regular tests that serve a diagnostic as well as or instead of an evaluative function;
- holding regular small-group tutorials.

You might also encourage your students to form study groups to help one another, although this does not solve the problem of teaching at an inappropriate level. It merely helps students cope with problems you have helped create.

Preparing for Large Classes

Let us assume that you have taken some of the foregoing advice into account, and you have now set your course objectives, written your course outline, worked out how you are going to evaluate your students, and prepared your lecture schedule. Now you are going to start preparing individual lectures.

Check out the classroom in which you will be teaching

Is it adequate to your needs? Does it have the technology you need? Obviously, you cannot prepare your lecture using that slick new presentation program if you are working in a room that has no data-projection capacity. You may very well find that you are being asked to do a job without being given the tools to do it properly, and that you have to become a champion of adequately equipped rooms in which to teach. Ideas on equipment needed in classrooms for different class sizes can be found in the last section of this guide.

Talk nicely to the technical support people who provide and maintain the equipment in the room

Get them to show you what it can do and how to use it, and ask them what they think would improve the room. They are your allies, and usually a terrific resource.

While you are preparing your lectures, think about the room and how you are going to use it

Some aspects of room use are going to require pre-planning. For example, if you have two overhead projectors and screens, which I recommend for large classes, how are you going to use them? I like to use one that I do not change very often during a class for outlines and larger ideas and another that changes much more frequently for more detailed work. Some instructors even like to block their lectures as a director might block a play, figuring out when they are going to leave the lectern or overhead projector and go walkabout, or where they will stand or sit to ask questions or generate discussion. Movement by the lecturer is certainly desirable. If it is not something that comes naturally to you, you might want to consider and indicate in your notes to yourself when it would be safe and effective for you to leave the lectern or overhead projector and venture out into the crowd. You might also consider how far you want to venture: up the centre aisle (which large classrooms should always have)? up the side aisles? right to the back? Doing this reminds those students who prefer to hide at the back of the class that they are neither invisible nor inaudible.

You can use the blackboard for numbers up to 200 or so if you are careful to make your writing big and clear, but you will have to plan how you will lay things out. Let the spatial arrangement on the board reflect the relations among the things you write there. And check sight lines to ensure that all the students can see all of the board work. Many chalkboards are not evenly lit, and some areas will not be clearly visible to some students regardless of how large your letters are.

Prepare, prepare and over-prepare

Although there may be some subjects that allow some instructors to take wing and soar free without a safety net, there are many more that will leave even the best performers prey to the fate of Icarus.

Organization must be seen to be done

Organize your material thoroughly, and provide students with a clear outline of what you will cover. It is easier for them to make sense of the information if they know where it is going and how topics inter-relate. It is not enough for organization to be done: it has to be seen to be done. Provide students with an outline, a conceptual map, of the day's class, either on an overhead or other projected image, or on the board. It is a good idea to leave this up for a significant part of the class so students can see where you are and can use the outline to help organize their notes. Anxiety and uncertainty about how things fit together or connect gets in the way of learning.

Have more material ready than you think you can use

You can always drop stuff that you have prepared, but you may not be able to come up with additional points if you get through your material too quickly. Mark your lecture notes to indicate the material that is essential, the material to drop if you are going more slowly than you anticipated, and optional material to include if you are going too quickly.

Remember that you can teach only two or three big ideas, if that much, in a single short class

This seems to be true of any class, and is especially true in large ones. First, you will have to slow down a little because you have to use more examples to reach a more diverse group of students. Second, you are also slowed down because redundancy, always a virtue in the classroom, becomes a cardinal virtue in a large class. Plan to follow the age-old scheme of telling students what you are going to tell them, telling them, and then telling them what you told them.

Handouts may be helpful, but consider some alternatives

If in large classes you have to scale down content somewhat, what can you do to make up for the uncovered material? Here the help offered in the literature on teaching large classes is fraught with problems. One common suggestion is to prepare full handouts to convey the factual matter, content of overheads, and other material we may want the students to have but do not want to spend too much time on in class. Alternatively, it is possible to prepare "partial handouts" with blank spaces on them which students can fill in with their own notes. Another approach is to put our lecture notes or necessary supporting material on reserve in the library, and one writer even suggests that we hire a senior student or graduate student to come to the classes and take detailed notes which can then be made available to students.

While all of these ideas may be helpful to students, they also present problems in a period of shrinking budgets and diminishing resources. For a start, the extensive use of handouts to convey material is problematic on the grounds of expense and ecology. Hectares of soft-woods are sacrificed to academic expediency, and intolerable strain is put on the already stretched or broken budgets of departments and students. Indeed, many departments have already severely curtailed or eliminated free course handouts, and one result is the increasingly popular practice of putting together relatively expensive packages of course materials that are sold to augment already very expensive texts.

I have no doubt that in some cases such uses of money and trees can be justified, but this is hardly a complete solution. Nor is putting material on reserve in the library when hundreds of students could be enrolled in a single course section. A significant number of them may want to consult those materials in the last few days before a test or final exam — exams that are often more heavily weighted than in the past because of the difficulties of evaluating by other means, such as essays, as student numbers increase.

While such problems seem impossible to eliminate, there are low-tech and high-tech means that at least may alleviate them. These include course bulletin boards, computer labs, and self-instructional packages.

It can help to post course notes in strategically positioned display cases, for instance close to the lecture hall or the professor's office. So can using either an electronic bulletin board or web page, or making the material available in a campus computer lab where students can download it on to their own disks. These days it is simple enough to provide material in a format that would make it usable by virtually all students on their own machine or one available at a university computing lab. Let us not forget, though, that this takes up a teacher's time and energy, and should be one more among the many things factored into determining the workload of those teaching really large classes.

Once we have got students into the computing lab, we might want to get them working at some interactive self-instructional packages, which provide another partial solution to the problems posed above. These too require the investment of resources and usually the involvement of a team of at least two: a teacher who determines the instructional objectives and content, and a programmer who can assist with the design and writing of the package. Working through such material can be (but need not be) made mandatory, and can be very effective because the interactivity can to some degree compensate for the large class experience where passive learning is too often the rule. I suggest that in courses where there are not regular small-group tutorials, scheduled computer tutorials can play an enormously important role, especially in the presence of a teaching assistant thoroughly conversant with your course material.

Plan in detail and in advance any interactive exercises you will use, including the specific questions you will ask or tasks you will assign

Do not rely on the spur of the moment to fill in the part of your lecture notes that just says "Discuss" or "Questions." Prepare questions carefully. I find the ones that work best are those to which there is a range of answers and those that require students to think and apply knowledge rather than merely to display knowledge. Such questions have the potential to make all students work and to have several of them give good answers. Well designed questions will also function diagnostically, so that you can learn what parts of your material need to be reviewed. Otherwise you run the risk of finding out that you taught something poorly only when students write the final exam.

Further suggestions for dealing with questions and answers and specific interactive techniques for large classes are given in the next part of the guide, where I pay particular attention to deign and use of effective questions.

Make sure that everything works before class

Try things out in the actual classroom. Often a videotape that plays well on your home machine will have glitches in sound or visual image when projected on a large screen. Your local technical support people can often help overcome such problems. If you are using either audiotape or videotape, the numbers on counters usually vary radically, and it is risky to rely on them to help you find material quickly. It is very easy to lose the attention and even the goodwill of a large class if you have minutes of down-time while you search for the needed clip. It is far more efficient to edit material on to tapes that contain only the material you will be using, provided this does not infringe copyright. If you are using a laserdisc, make sure the player gives you the capacity to do the things you need, like chapter searches or freeze frames. If it does not, you may have to edit this material on to videotape. Again, you should be careful to check with your audiovisual centre that your use of taped materials is permissible under Canadian copyright law.

Be prepared for the moment when technology fails you

As classes get larger, you tend to become not only more dependent on technology, but also on more sophisticated technology. Always be prepared to step down one technological level. For instance, if you are teaching a class of 150 students and are planning to use overheads, you can always go to the board on that special occasion when all of your overhead bulbs blow or someone has thoughtlessly moved the whole machine to another room. In a class of 600, when the computer or data projector is down and all of those hours with the presentation program have come to nought, you can step down to overheads, but only if you have prepared them or, less satisfactorily, at least have brought some blanks and overhead pens with you.

Secure an annual course budget to acquire audio and visual and other course materials

Typically, departments are trying to save money by introducing large sections, but the instructor of such a section still needs the right tools to do the job well. Often that includes specialized equipment for the room (described in the section on the well-equipped classroom) and other educational materials for class presentations. These materials may be expensive, take quite a while to track down and acquire, and they will probably need to be updated regularly. Administrators with an eye on the bottom line need to be convinced that they cannot arrive at that line as quickly as they might like, and the special needs of large classes may have to be explained and defended.

If your class is large enough, every student problem comes up every year. Be prepared

For every exam you make up, you may as well prepare at least one supplemental exam. Personal crises will routinely arise — deaths in the family, the aftermath of broken relationships, sexual assault and harassment, pregnancies and abortions, financial problems that affect your students' ability to continue at university, learning disabilities demanding a variety of accommodations. Bear in mind that you are no expert in dealing with these things, and that you should be ready to refer students to the appropriate services on campus. Do not take on these problems yourself.

Have a clear policy on late and deferred assignments, on missed exams, plagiarism, and so on, and communicate those policies clearly to the class at the beginning of the year and again later as appropriate. Students should know in advance the penalties for missed and late work, and what sorts of documentation they will require to get deferrals for assignments and permission to do make-up tests or other exercises.

Delivering the Lecture
Things to do in the Classroom

Classroom Strategies And Behaviours

Much of what follows is predicated on the belief that we should try, as much as possible, to preserve in large classes the qualities that make small class instruction so valuable. Students should feel involved in, excited by, and take responsibility for their own learning. The classroom should be inclusive of all its members. Students should be treated as individuals and should have an opportunity to test their own ideas and opinions so as to affect their teachers and classmates. And students should have reasonable access to their teachers.

Energy, passion, and intensity

This subject has been discussed in theory above, but putting ideas into practice is another story. Think about what gets you motivated to teach your class, and develop a routine. The energy you will need for teaching varies directly with the size of the class, so you may need to program what you do beforehand and afterwards to allow for that. I like to reserve time before and after class, so that I can build up my energy at the start and have time to recover later. I typically come out of teaching a large class exhausted and in need of some down time.

I like to spend the hour before class imagining my performance and going over my notes so that I hardly have to look at them in class, if at all. To remind myself that it really is a performance, and that I am about to play a role in the lecture theatre, I usually say "show-time" to myself just as I am about to begin, often while I am rolling up my sleeves as another means of reminding myself of how hard I now have to work. I find that it also helps if I remember that my passion comes from my love for my subject. I can perform with less restraint when I remember that it is my discipline and not just me that is being represented. It is important for students to see how profoundly enjoyable it is for me to engage with these materials both in the short and long terms. Wear your heart on your sleeve.

Quite naturally, there will be days when you are tired, sick, depressed, frustrated, overworked, or otherwise do not feel up to the demands that the large class makes of you. On those days, you might try remembering that, like it or not, in a large class you are a performer playing a part. You are not just yourself — although of course you are always that too. When such days come, and they will, do not apologize or make excuses to the class in advance but try to do an impersonation of your better self. Your students will appreciate it, and you will feel good about yourself at the end of the day.

When even that fails, as it sometimes will, and you give a dull, uninspiring, less-than-fully-lucid-and-coherent class, try to figure out what you could have done to have avoided those specific problems and make notes so you will remember next time, and try not to let it adversely affect future classes. Students are very forgiving and it is in their interests that we perform well.

Setting the tone and starting the class

How you begin classes is crucial to their success, and the start often comes well before you open your mouth to lecture. Many instructors of large classes have had success with one or both of the following:

Setting tone

i. Play music, if possible music that is appropriate to the day's subject, as the students are coming into class. Beyond setting tone or creating atmosphere, stopping the music is also a clear signal to the students that the more formal part of the class is now beginning.

ii. Have something up on the overhead to focus or challenge the students' interest. This can be just about anything that is relevant to the day's material: a cartoon, an outline of the lecture, relevant and provocative quotations, a newspaper article or excerpts, a problem, etc.

Starting the class

Getting the attention of a large and typically raucous group of undergraduates is a challenge in itself, and done badly can ruin the tone of a class and even alienate your students. Therefore do not start your class with intimidation or demands that students shut up. On the other hand, it is fair to set ground rules for your class, and I set out the following ones at the beginning of the year and reinforce them periodically as needed.

*   When the music stops, class begins: it is time to be quiet.
*   If you are late, please enter by the doors at the back of the class and find a seat quickly to minimize disruption to the rest of the class.
*   If you know you must leave early, choose an appropriate seat close to an exit.
*   If you want to listen to music on your personal stereo, read a newspaper, or catch up on reading for this or other courses, there are better places to do these things than in class.
*   Just because the class is big does not mean that you are invisible or inaudible. Common courtesy is expected.

Make clear when and where students can get in contact with you. Set limits on when they can phone you, lest you be telephoned at 2 a.m. on the night before the exam or before that big assignment is due. It happens.

Here are a few ways of starting the class.

- After checking equipment and sorting your notes, stand at your lectern and check the microphone. That alone will get the students' attention. Then wait until there is silence before continuing.
- Start by greeting them in more or less the same way each time, so that they come to recognize this signal. This could be something as simple as "Hi, we are going to start now," or "Hello and here we go again." Once more, wait for silence after the greeting. If you start lecturing while students are still talking among themselves, they will get the signal that such behaviour is acceptable.
- Use some mechanical device (ringing a small handbell, dimming the lights in the room, putting on or changing the transparency) to signal the start of the lecture. Then wait for silence.

Mobility and body language

Large classes typically place barriers between lecturers and students, beginning with physical distance, which in turn exacerbates psychological distance. Lecterns, projectors for overheads, video, data or slides, that put you and the class more or less in the dark, desks or demonstration tables, hard-wired microphones, even dependence on your notes, come between you and your students. To make the classroom experience more intimate and effective, to create a stronger connection between teacher and class, try to break these down. When possible, move away from your apparatus, out from behind the barriers, and remove the distinction between the teacher's space and the students' space, especially when you are asking questions or trying to lead a discussion. In those latter instances, sitting on the desk, moving towards or away from questioners or respondents signal that you are ceding your control of the classroom to your students and making space for them to participate.

When doing these things, or even when lecturing, remember to embrace the whole class. Most teachers favour one side of the room over the other, which is easy to cure once we are aware of it. Do not be afraid to work the aisles, the sides, even the back of the room. I find that it wakes students up and makes them more attentive when they have to turn their heads to follow you around the room. The energy of your body language, particularly including your hand gestures and larger movements, helps to emphasize ideas and keep the class lively. You should not try to disappear into the chalkboard, standing immobile with your back to it, arms and legs crossed in a gesture that closes you off entirely from the class, or remain glued to the lectern or overhead. But neither can you be a whirling dervish, moving too frantically around the room, or a constant pacer, wearing a lateral track in the floor at the front of the room and lecturing predominantly to the side walls. There is a balance of movement and stasis that will be determined by a combination of your own personality and the nature of specific elements of your presentation on any given day.

Many lecturers who are new to the profession or the large class will initially (and naturally) feel most secure at the lectern with their notes right in front of them. In general, if you need your notes you should use them, and not sacrifice a coherent lecture to a perceived need to perambulate. On the other hand, weaning yourself from a dependence on those notes can set you free to be more dynamic. You can do this gradually by indicating in the margin of your text those parts of the lecture that you are most comfortable with, and where you can make brief forays from your lectern-position of power and authority. You might find it easier to do this when telling an anecdote, or giving examples, or initiating discussion, rather than for units of the lecture that deal with relatively complex materials. Eventually you will develop more lecture units, even complex parts — set pieces as it were — that allow you the freedom to roam.

Physical facts

Remember that everything has to be bigger than normal. If you are writing on the board, write big (you might even get oversized chalk); check if writing on the board can be seen. If your class has more than 125 students you probably should not be using the board at all. For classes up to 400 you can use ordinary transparencies, but beyond that you will have to move to super-bright overhead, video and data projectors, and probably to presentation programs that allow you to present a variety of images and text in a large and dramatic way. Your educational or faculty development office should be able to help you with these techniques, and a growing number of user-friendly presentation programs are available. See the last section of this guide on the properly equipped classroom.

You will also need to amplify your voice for classes over 125, and for some people even for classes smaller than that. If you are in any doubt about your need for a microphone, err in the direction of caution and use one. At the very least, it widens the dynamic range of your voice in the classroom, enabling you to speak softly or loudly to underscore your points and to provide variety in your lectures. It is also crucial that the microphone be wireless, so that you can be dynamic in movement as well as in voice, and can be heard throughout the classroom even when you are away from a central position at the lectern.

It is not just your equipment that has to be bigger and better; so do you. Remember that small hand or facial gestures or minor changes in inflection will be imperceptible to people at the back of the room. Make large gestures, do not be afraid to act your heart out. Be bigger than you are, which is not as difficult as it might sound, but do not let it go to your head.

Teaching through the senses

People remember in different ways, or favour different senses, some learning best through visual cues, some through auditory ones; some are particularly affected by spatial cues, or by a combination of sensory data. The power of tapping into students' preferred ways of learning was demonstrated to me one day while reviewing a complex term I had introduced in the previous class. I pointed to the blank space on the board where the term had been written and several students nodded their heads in understanding as the spatial cue triggered their memories. Since then I have been more careful in determining the spatial relationships among things on my overheads and board work as a means of helping these spatial learners. I have also often wished there was a way to tap into olfactory memory, which is very powerful. I have joked about creating a scratch-and-sniff anthology of English literature, with sulphur and brimstone scratch patches for the descent to hell in *Paradise Lost*, for instance. I eagerly await the technology that will allow us to waft timely and relevant odours through our classrooms.

Dale Roy of McMaster University has also grappled with this issue, and uses the following exercise in a course on lecturing. When getting faculty to develop a good set of overheads he asks them to create two transparencies on the same topic — one text-based and the other to take the form of an image or picture. Participants then take the pairs of overheads into a lecture theatre and each person speaks briefly about each one. Without fail, the audience is later able to reconstruct the talk based on the image (and even reconstruct the image), but can barely remember more than 50% of the text-based overhead and talk. Dale concludes that for many people pictures really are worth a thousand words and we need to make use of that knowledge.

Repetition and variation

As Samuel Johnson observed, people need to be reminded much more often than they need to be informed: we rarely learn things we have been told only once. In large classes, repetition with variation is essential, particularly when the variation appeals to another sense. This can be done in two ways. First, use everything you can to teach through sound and sight: the board and projection devices, body language, writing things down, even saying stuff out loud together, preferably in a light-hearted way. Certain motifs (like important definitions of terms, or major ideas in the course) should recur in the same form of words until they become at once an in-joke and a mnemonic device.

The second way you can use repetition with variety lies in the choice of examples you will use in large classes, and is predicated on the fact that the student body we face today is more culturally, ethnically, and educationally diverse than it was before. Add to this the fact that the students in your class are there for a variety of reasons, and will use your course materials in quite different ways, and you have some idea of the challenge that faces you when you try to reach or connect with most of them, when you try to use an example that will strike them with force and clarity. The single analogy or example will no longer suffice, and you will have to develop a battery of alternatives, and to keep them current, which is admittedly difficult. Here the entire responsibility need not devolve on you. Rather, coming up with useful analogies and examples to explain something is an excellent way to involve the class itself. Ask students to think of their own analogies, examples, or applications. They will generally recognize their common cause with us and respond well when we confess difficulty with some aspect of an explanation and ask for help. Indeed, anything you can do that will encourage students to take more responsibility for their own learning is a good thing.

It is also highly appropriate to stay current with what knowledge your students bring to the class, since educational background and ability can be very diverse in large classes and having some idea of what your students know can drive your choice of examples or illustrations. Ask them what ideas they already have, whether they studied this topic before. What Shakespeare play did they read in high school? Did they see such-and-such a film? Did they do Fourier transforms in a previous course?

Variety in instructional method

There are among us some rhapsodes who can, through intellectual, oratorical, and dramatic gifts, and a certain charisma, fly high through lectures without the safety net of notes and extensive preparation. Those talented individuals are probably able to hold the attention of their students with straight lecturing right through the hour, and perhaps even for a second hour, although that is much more difficult. But if this is all they do, even that performance will have lost some of its force through simple familiarity and habituation well before a single semester is over. In lecturing and learning, as in many other aspects of life, variety spurs our appetites.

Conventional wisdom on this subject advises us to change our method of delivery every 15-20 minutes, and we need to do so more for our students' sake than for ourselves. While this often involves activities or techniques that are discipline-specific, there are two fundamental strategies that apply across different subject matter. We can change the medium of instruction, for instance from lecturing to using pre-recorded material (video, slides). This can help us by providing a break from lecturing while we recoup our energies, but the students still remain passive or unengaged learners. To overcome that condition, we need to introduce some type of interactive or student-centred exercises. A brief period of small group discussion, voting on alternatives, writing a brief summary of part of a lecture, all these approaches change what students do and are likely to result in a spike in learning, attention, and engagement. Some specific exercises suitable for large classes, including some tips on asking questions and responding to answers, are given in the section on Interactive Methods below.

Eye contact

Non-verbal communication is crucial in large classes where there is not time to speak with each student individually. Looking directly at your students, especially seeing them singly, is an important means of making a personal connection with them, of establishing your awareness of them as individuals. In large classes professors typically tend to do a quick radar sweep across the crowded room, registering a mass of more or less undifferentiated bodies. We look across the tops of the heads of the people in the back row, or stare abstracted into space, ready to pluck from it that rarefied and pure idea. I am not suggesting that we eliminate those behaviours. But we should add to them the ability to make sustained eye contact with individual students, held long enough to let that person know that you are engaging with her or him, that you care about whether or not they are with you. Through practice, I have found that I can comfortably make 20 or 25 such connections in a 50-minute class. And almost always those students will acknowledge the connection. They will smile, or nod their heads. They will also be more likely to speak with you before or after class or during your office hours. This simple technique thus has big payoffs in interpersonal and other ways, the most important of which is discussed next.

Reading the class

Making individual eye contact allows you to read the faces of your students, and to know immediately whether things are working or not. It enables you to do a quick check when you see someone looking puzzled or put off by something you have just said. In big classes, you have to read very small signs, partly because the pressure of being in a group so large inhibits most students from confessing their ignorance or non-understanding. Where confusion is registered on a student's face, chances are that a whole lot of others are confused too. It is possible of course that you are looking at a particularly obtuse or ill-prepared student, but it is just as likely that you have explained something badly or inadequately. Perhaps the students need more background, lack some fundamental knowledge that would make the day's subject comprehensible.

We do well to remember that we do not know what or how to teach unless we have some sense of what our students know and do not know. We are always making a compromise between teaching a class and teaching subject matter, and when we read puzzlement on student faces, we should find out what the class is lacking that day. There is no point in raking students or their previous instructors over the coals for inadequate preparation. Within reasonable limits (there are some students who for one reason or another should not be there), it is your problem now. In those circumstances, I take the responsibility on myself. I say, "You look puzzled. Where in what I was saying did the problems arise? Did I leave something out?" Or "I have explained this badly. Let me have another go at it," or some such formulation. Students seem to appreciate this, and are subsequently encouraged to speak up when other difficulties arise. They also seem to understand that what you have offered is sometimes a polite fiction that enables you to do what is really remedial work without calling it that. Of course it is also always possible that you did explain the thing badly. Enough said.

Humour

If you have it, use it. Educators and cultural theorists (and even Mary Poppins) have known for a very long time that delight and instruction go together, so if you cannot be funny, at least be good-humoured. Let students see that you enjoy what you are doing and what you are talking about, that you want to be in the classroom with them. This will sometimes be a challenge, because there will be students in your class who are unprepared or inattentive. But dealing with them harshly can leave a bitter taste in everyones' mouths. Approaching these difficulties in a good-humoured way will usually be more productive. For instance, when I suspect that students have not done the reading for the day's class I ask them to do one of two things, depending on the type of text they are using. If it is a paperback, I ask them to hold their copies up so I can see the spines, and then comment on their pristine, uncracked or virginal nature. For hardcovers, I ask them to open them to the page under consideration, and listen for the chiropractic spine cracks of texts never opened to that page before. We all have a little laugh, the point has been made, and public and social pressure can be applied without humiliating anyone.

Performing your material

To do this, you will have to shed some inhibitions and maybe even some preconceptions of what a professor is, although it is also true that many of the instructors assigned to teach large classes are among the less inhibited, more flamboyant members of departments. If the material gives you joy, if teaching it gives you pleasure, then let that show. Do not be afraid to let students laugh at you and your foibles and enthusiasms: let them show too.

Self-revelation

I am not suggesting that you do a physical or psychic striptease for them, but students love to know a bit of the personality and personal history of their teachers. If you can be a bit cryptic about this so much the better — as in what I call the "as-I-know-to-my-personal-cost" syndrome, particularly useful when teaching something like a love poem with a rejected suitor, or generally or specifically talking about ways in which research can go wrong. We may find ourselves dull (after all we have hung around ourselves for a long time now), but students are curious about our own educations and interests, our research work, or any other details of our personal and professional lives. Obviously there are limits to what we should say, and I am not suggesting that we pass into our anecdotages. But appropriately chosen and placed revelations can leaven a lecture in much the same way that humour can, and bring about a peak in the level of student interest on to which you can build some real learning.

A number of lecturers in large classes solicit brief written biographies by students at the beginning of the course as a way of personalizing the large class experience. This is most effective when the lecturer also participates in the exercise, and distributes to all members of the class her or his own brief biography, including selected personal and professional details.

Ending the class

Just as starting the large class presents some special problems, so does finishing it, and it is very easy to lose the effect of anything you do in the last five minutes. In a large class the commotion and unrest caused by dozens or hundreds of students packing up to leave is very disruptive to those still trying to listen and learn. To minimize this:

- Avoid saying things like, "One or two more points and then we can all go." You may as well say "Start packing up now."

- Try not to leave the question period as the last thing in class. You will inhibit questions and invite restlessness. Rather, use the last few minutes to recap the important points, and to look forward to the next class, or to talk about assignments or tests.
- Do not always go on until the last moment. Stop a minute or two early from time to time, so that there is some element of the unpredictable.

Starting and finishing on time

If you habitually start late, students will come late. If you habitually finish late, students will start to leave before you have finished. Besides, many of them will have classes in remote parts of the campus, and they need the time between classes, as might the next instructor using your classroom, who will have her or his own things to get ready. What you have to say is not more important than what other instructors have to say, and you have no right to impinge on their time. Bear in mind also that in large classes just moving a lot of bodies in and out of the room takes quite a while, and then it takes the students more time still to find their friends and seats, and settle. Students need those ten minutes between classes.

Erasing your boards, tidying your junk

No one comes in between classes to clean up after us, and the next instructor coming in appreciates being able to get right to work without having to undo or put right your mess.

Interactive Methods:

General Practices And Strategies

Perhaps the biggest challenge for the teacher of large classes is to help students feel that they are involved, have a stake in their own education, that they and their opinions and beliefs can make a difference. If you plan to do something other than just lecturing all year, if you plan to let students get involved in classes, that has to be factored into every aspect of the course and its design, from staffing and course objectives to methods of evaluation and the plans for individual lectures. The following strategies and techniques aim to make students feel that they are involved in the class and that their concerns and questions are being addressed.

Begin as you mean to go on

I am a firm believer in the principle that you should begin as you mean to go on. If you want to involve students, it is far easier to start doing that in the first few classes than it is to lecture for a month and then start looking for participation. Start the year, then, by asking questions that have many correct answers, and that have small or short answers. For instance, when I introduce my course by quickly going through the syllabus at the first meeting, I make it a habit to ask questions about what students know, what they have already covered. As discussed earlier, I do not assume that this year's class knows what last year's class knew or has covered the same works.

Not only does this afford students a relatively risk-free way to participate and the professor a quick means of diagnosing this class's knowledge and deficiencies, but it also makes clear that he or she cares about and intends to serve the educational needs of this particular group. I find little value in criticising a class or its former teachers for what has not been learned. If I discover pockets of ignorance in places where I expected to find the foundation material for my course, it does very little good for me to build splendid palaces of high-sounding thought without doing some site preparation first. This is not confined to the opening class or classes, but continues as I deal with new material or concepts throughout the course.

Asking questions

Early in the year (and later too), ask especially those questions to which there can be a range of correct or more-or-less correct answers. This lets lots of students speak, and encourages self-confidence. For instance, instead of asking a class what the coefficient of friction is, you might ask for a range of situations or conditions in which it would be appropriate to use it. Remember that your questions must be carefully prepared to achieve your intended purposes.

Ray Rasmussen is particularly helpful on this subject in his *Practical discussion techniques for instructors* (Rasmussen, 1984). Here Rasmussen categorises questions on the basis of their cognitive level, divergence or convergence, structure, and straightforwardness.

Generally speaking, **high cognitive level questions** that require the operations of analysis, synthesis, and evaluation work better than low level questions that require only rote memory or simple restatement of materials. A low level question might elicit the name of a character in a book, while a high level question might ask about the functions of that character. A **divergent question** indicates that there are a number of plausible answers, which makes it safer for students to offer their responses and is thus often preferable to a convergent question that calls for a single right answer.

Unstructured questions (e.g. "What did you think of this book?") are wide open and require time to formulate an answer. It is often better to use **structured questions** (e.g. "What are some things that affected your emotional response to the story?") which deal with specific issues or aspects of the subject matter and generate quicker, more focused answers. On the whole, **straightforward or single questions** are preferable to multiple, often nested questions, interspersed with information that make students unsure of what is being asked of them.

The amount of time you wait for answers after asking a question is also crucial. Most instructors tend to quickly answer their own questions if they do not get an immediate response. A good rule of thumb is to wait 7-10 seconds or longer, and if no response is forthcoming, ask the students if they would like more time to think, or if they would like the question restated. You can also create an expectation of longer wait times by telling students that you will give them a minute to think before taking answers. Do not get in the very counterproductive habit of answering your own questions, or of staring expectantly at the one or two students who habitually answer.

Extending the number of students actively *engaged* in learning is the goal of these exercises, and Rasmussen points out that this is not the same thing as *participation*. He argues that learners are active when they are engaged in thinking about or discussing course issues, but that this does not necessarily involve one-to-one exchanges between teacher and student. Suggestions for other types of activating exercises are given below.

Responding to questions and comments

When responding to questions and answers, be gentle and helpful. Make sure you understand the answer or the question, and that you do not turn either into what you would like to hear. Take the time to check by repeating what the student has said to the whole class and asking if you have accurately reported what they said. In almost every instance you will have to do this in a large class anyway because the odds are excellent that most students did not hear what was said. You are the only one facing the whole class and the only one equipped with a microphone. If you do not repeat what was said, you run the risk of losing the attention of the rest of the class as you engage in a discussion with a few students who are typically sitting in the first three rows. If you have a student with a strong voice that can be heard by the whole class, you can save yourself the trouble of repeating what is said by moving counter-intuitively. That is, instead of moving towards the speaker, move away so that she or he has to speak loudly to reach you.

You do not have to answer all of the questions or respond to all of the answers yourself. You can ask the rest of the class if they agree with a particular response, or if they can answer the question another student asked. Teaching students that they can learn from one another is perhaps more valuable than teaching them directly, although it always takes more time to learn through discussion. It is important to note that not all of that discussion has to take place in class. Get students to introduce themselves to those sitting nearby, help them form study groups by setting up group sign-up sheets, arranging places and times for meetings, and suggesting topics or specific materials for discussion. Students who study and work together learn more than those who do not.

Find what is useful in any response. Even when someone is entirely out to lunch, try to account for why they might have gone wrong in that particular way and explain it. Never bullshit. If you do not know the answer to a question you are asked, admit it. Ask if anyone else in the class knows. Tell the students that you will find out for the next class (and do so!). You might even ask the student who asked the question to try to find out too, and then compare notes just before the next class begins.

There are two things to keep in mind here. The first is that people who ask tough or very specialized questions sometimes have very specialized knowledge, and they may know some corner of your field better than you do because of a particular interest or experience. They will know that you are faking it, and can then undermine whatever confidence the class may have built up in you. The second thing is that even if the questioner is genuinely in the dark about this issue, someone else or several people in this large group may very well know the answer. There are a lot of brains and a lot of specific knowledge and experience in a large class.

Using students' personalities

Try to discover and use the personalities of different students in the class. Where some students can be seen as individuals with whom you can banter, exchange jokes or whatever, all can be seen as individuals. There will always be some students who declare their natures early and often, and who will have particular and easily identifiable interests or attitudes that they regularly parade before the class. You can use these traits, refer to them even before that student has spoken or offered to speak. If you can learn some names, even better, as this shows that you are interested in people as individuals. Do not be daunted by the fact that you cannot learn all of the names — better to learn some than none. Get students to announce their names when they ask questions or answer them. You may not remember them, but it shows that you care who they are, that you wish to see the class as individuals. This also gives students the chance to identify their classmates, and might make them more likely to talk about the course outside class.

Fostering a community of learners

Encourage the class to think of itself as a group with a common cause. Suggest to students that they organize study groups to discuss the course material together out of class, and even help them to do so. Explain that we are all (including lecturers and teaching assistants) working through this material together. In-jokes, those based on common experiences within the course or on the personalities of those in the course, are very useful, so long as we are careful not to humiliate or victimize anyone. Used well, they create an awareness of the class as group, sharing a special or unique experience.

Ombuddies

Ombuddies (my preferred form, much friendlier than "ombudspersons") are a way of finding out what is working and what is not in large classes. For a variety of reasons students are often reluctant to complain directly to the instructor about problems that they perceive in any course, and the seeming remoteness of the professor in a large class exacerbates their hesitancy to come forward. One way to overcome this problem is to have designated student representatives that speak for other class members.

Early in the year, explain the function of ombuddies (mainly to act as conduits between the students and the professor), and ask for volunteers. They can either change after one term, or stay in the job all year. You will want at least three and maybe more in a large class, to ensure that at least one representative is there for every class.

Give them badges or buttons so they can be identified by their classmates, and re-introduce them periodically to encourage the class to speak with them. Take the ombuddies out for coffee or tea from time to time, and talk about how the course is going. Even if no one has spoken to them, they will still give you some interesting comments. Sometimes, I suspect, they tell you what they think and attribute it to others, but that's fine. They are part of the class too, you are getting the feedback you need, and you are getting it when you need it, not just on a student evaluation form at the end of the year when it is too late to do anything about the problems.

Question and suggestion boxes

Suggestion boxes provide another means of getting feedback from the class as you go along rather than waiting until the end of the year. Encourage students periodically (not just once at the beginning of the year) to comment and make suggestions about the conduct of the course in general and on specific points. Have them submit questions related to the course material — students often do not get a chance, or are reluctant, to ask questions during class. A question/suggestion box allows them to drop those questions off at the end or beginning of a session. You should make it a matter of routine to empty the box at the end of each class, and take up at least some of the questions, as appropriate, in the next class. Remember that eye contact is interaction too. Not all exchanges have to be verbal for both parties to experience some kind of connection.

Difficult students

Dealing with the difficult, obtrusive, or demanding student can be especially problematic in a large class where time for participation is at a premium. But by virtue of numbers alone you are pretty much guaranteed at least one variety of loon per class. These students seem always ready to contribute to discussions with more or less wacky questions and answers, and will often have fellow classmates rolling their eyes as soon as they begin to speak.

Such students have to be dealt with gently, first for humane reasons and secondly lest you alienate or intimidate the whole class by treating one class member harshly. Two basic and easily implemented strategies for dealing with such individuals are available. The first is to make them invisible. After the student has been given one chance to speak in class, just do not see him or her any more. A large class gives you lots of places to look, and you can simply focus away from where you know that student will be sitting. A second approach is to notice the student, and explain very briefly that you would like to hear from other students first before letting anyone speak a second time. Or just say that you would like to hear from some new voices in this discussion. This acknowledges that student as a frequent contributor, which often seems to act as a salve for the person's feelings.

In extreme cases, you might take such students aside at the end of class, praise their willingness to participate, explain that you would like to give others who are more reticent a chance to speak, and that is the reason you will not be calling on them as often as they might like. Be gentle. You have a lot of power to hurt people, or to damage their self-esteem.

Interactive methods for large classes

The perceptive reader will have already realized that what I am trying to do in the large class is to recreate as much as possible some of the best qualities and aspects of small classes. Specifically I want to encourage interaction among students and professors, take into consideration the problems and insights of individual students, provide an opportunity for individuals to affect the agenda and outcomes of the class, and create a sense of a community of learners. I outline here a number of classroom-tested strategies and techniques that have been used to involve large groups of individuals in learning.

The first principle is that not all learning has to go through the professor. The corollary to this is that the professor does not have to comment on or respond to every utterance by a student. Two types of large-class interactive exercises that go beyond basic questioning and answering flow from this principle. One is based on gathering a range of responses in a batch without stopping to comment on individual contributions, and the other is based on the principle that if they cannot all talk to you, at least they can talk to each other.

Gathering a range of responses in a batch

Brainstorming can be used in a number of ways, the simplest of which is just gathering ideas about approaches or solutions to an issue or problem. It can also be used more specifically as a means of diagnosing the general level of students' knowledge of a subject, introducing new material, and even for setting the pedagogic agenda for a unit of a course. Here is an example of a brainstorming exercise used in this way.

A subject or issue is announced to the class (e.g. acid rain, or poetic scansion, or the Vietnam war), and the class is asked for *anything that they know or have heard or read about that subject.* Typically, this will be done at the very beginning of a unit of a course or lecture on that subject. The instructor records on the board or overhead all of the things that are said, regardless of whether they are correct or not. You may comment on things offered, but you need not do so and it is best to keep these minimal. If possible, the instructor will *arrange or group* these things in appropriate columns or areas of the board or overhead.

When the class has nothing more to add, or when a time limit has been reached, *the instructor comments on the set of things* on the board. This can be done in a number of ways, and will naturally depend on how the instructor wishes to use the exercise. If it is an introduction and diagnostic, for instance, the instructor might comment on how much the class already knows about the subject, and point out which areas will receive further attention in future classes. At this point the instructor should also have a pretty good idea of how much this particular class knows. Furthermore, she or he will also know what misconceptions or misinformation may exist about this subject, and can begin to correct them at an early stage.

By having accepted all of the comments uncritically from the outset, at the point where the instructor is dealing with misconceptions there is a separation in time from the person who made the error. This spares that student possible public embarrassment and lowers the psychological temperature for students who participate.

The instructor can also draw attention to the arrangement or grouping of things on the board, and use the opportunity to give the big picture, to discuss the inter-relation of the elements of this subject that will be the subject of future classes. Finally, brainstorming, or finding out the ideas a class already has about a subject, can also be done in written form by means of short-answer or multiple-choice questions related to future course content. Responses can be taken up in subsequent classes.

Quescussion is a type of discussion that is conducted entirely in the form of questions. It was developed by Prof. Paul Bidwell of the English Department at the University of Saskatchewan where he has used it with great success in the teaching of poetry. It has proved to be very useful in handling a variety of subjects even, or perhaps especially, very controversial ones, and works across a wide range of class sizes. In large classes it is particularly useful because it allows a lot of students to make brief contributions without interventions by the professor, and because the exercise can be put to several uses. It works like this.

First, the instructor explains the rules of quescussion, which are:

- Everything said must be in the form of a question;
- Participants must wait until four (this number can vary with the size of the class) other people have spoken before they can speak again;
- Statements in the form of questions are not allowed (e.g. "All professors wear polyester, don't they?");
- If someone makes a statement, the rest of the class is to shout "Statement";
- The exercise is self-policing;

- No nasty *ad hominen* questions are to be directed to other speakers (e.g. "Isn't that the kind of question that a megalomaniacal fascist would ask?"). Typically, these turn out to be disguised statements and are inadmissible on those grounds too. This rule is often unnecessary, but will come into play if the subjects discussed are ones that people might have strong feelings about, such as politics, abortion, euthanasia, or religion.

Next, the instructor sets out the subject for the quescussion. This can be *a problem* to be solved or confronted (relatively complex ones are best, but obviously this has to be suited to the class). Problems can be ethical, philosophical, social, psychological, literary, mathematical, or scientific. The subject could also be in the form of a carefully formulated *provocative question or statement*, or *a text* of appropriate length and difficulty to be analyzed or discussed.

Then comes the quescussion itself, the length of which will vary with the task that has been set, but which will rarely last beyond 10 minutes and is more often in the five-minute range. Classes have to learn how to do quescussion well, and you can expect some silences between questions when you first use this exercise. Don't worry: they are thinking hard. One of the impressive things about this exercise is how quickly it climbs up Bloom's taxonomy and encourages quite difficult questions. Furthermore, people will try out ideas they would hesitate to express under other circumstances, largely I think because everything is tentative and provisional when it is expressed in the form of a question. It also helps that a heated exchange between two class members cannot develop because of the rule calling for intervening speakers.

How you choose to follow up this exercise can vary, from doing nothing to doing a great deal. If you choose to do nothing, and sometimes that will be the right thing, you have at least introduced your class to a range of questions on this subject. However, if you want to address some or all of the issues raised by the exercise, you can follow Prof. Bidwell's practice of tape-recording or videotaping the quescussion, transcribing all of the questions, and presenting them to the class as the focus for future discussion. Alternatively, you or your designate can record the questions on the board or overhead, grouping them if desired, and use them as a springboard to a traditional type of discussion or lecture.

The one-minute paper and other one-minute exercises are useful ways to get students to prepare short responses to a question, issue, or text, and to get ideas from several speakers in a short time. In the case of the one-minute paper students are given a brief period (it can be one, two, or three minutes but not longer) to write a one-sentence response on what they perceive to be the most important aspect of a particular topic or issue. This can be done individually, or with students working as pairs or threes, and when the designated time has elapsed a number of the responses are read to the whole class. Because the exercise is limited in time and in the amount students can say, the long speeches that some class members like to give are eliminated, and the responses tend to be more precise. As long as you do not respond to each individual point, a lot of viewpoints can be gathered quickly.

One way to follow up on this is to have some of the most useful responses written on to overheads or the board and used as a springboard for further lecturing or discussion. Singling out those good responses also assigns value to student contributions and encourages students to believe that their insights are important.

A variant on this approach is to divide a task or problem up into several parts and assign each one to various zones or sections of the class. Give students preparation time to work up a response, but with the instruction that their answer need not be comprehensive and cannot take more than a minute to present. Call for one or more responses from a class section and after one or more people have spoken for a minute on their part of the problem, other members of that group can add supplementary information. Then move on to the next group until all sections have been represented. This technique can work with the analysis of all kinds of texts (theoretical, critical, and literary texts), with slides and film stills, and with many kinds of conceptual and practical problems.

Large group role playing or mass debate, which pits one large section of the class in debate/discussion with one or more other sections, can be a very liberating way to encourage broad interaction and participation in a large class. The instructor assigns opposing positions to different groups of students, regardless of what side of the issue students might choose to take as individuals. Naturally, the assignments will vary with the discipline and specific subject, and the oppositions could be political, ideological, theoretical, moral, ethical, philosophical, methodological, interpretive, etc. In a large class dealing with a complex issue you can of course use more than two positions for groups to present.

The exercise works best when the subject or topic for debate is announced and the problem introduced in appropriate detail in a previous class. At that time you can assign roles so that students have time to think about a particular side of the controversy or issue, or you can ask them to think generally about all sides of the issue without assigning specific roles. You can also give pointers to some relevant reading. The debate or discussion seems to work best when the various positions are defined in quite polar terms. The reason for this seems to be that when assigned positions are extreme, students are less likely to fear that their arguments might be mistaken for genuinely held beliefs.

The instructor begins by setting out the question or issue for debate in whatever detail is required, and then acts as moderator. Once the discussion gets going, stand back a little. Do not respond to what the speakers say: let them speak to and challenge one another. Your role is partly that of the speaker of the house, identifying the next to speak and loosely monitoring behaviour, and partly guide, intervening briefly, occasionally, and strategically to keep the discussion along profitable lines without stifling some of the levity that almost always comes with this exercise.

This type of discussion can run for quite a while, and has its own energy. It involves some risk since debates rely on substantial student input and goodwill, and you have to be deft enough to steer proceedings a little from time to time. Doing the debriefing that should follow the mass debate requires agility too. But a bit of danger can spice up your teaching and raise your energy level. There always seem to be enough people who like to speak in a large group, and I have had some terrific classes that were structured around this type of activity.

Taking big chances by relying on the more or less unpredictable contributions of others can lead to the best and most exciting classes. It can, of course, also lead to the worst and most embarrassing situations. What I mean by taking big chances in this context is in devising classes that use student participation to achieve course objectives, instead of just lecturing. Using the sorts of teaching approaches described here takes imagination and even daring, but the payoff is large for instructor and students.

There are some important principles to bear in mind when planning participatory exercises. First, the task and issue have to be very clearly defined. Vague questions and unclear procedures are deadly. Secondly, students have to feel safe to participate freely, and to be able to take reasonable risks with what they say. And instructors must remember that they do not have to respond themselves to everything that every student says.

Independent discussion groups

One rationale for having students discuss issues among themselves is that if they cannot all talk to you, at least they can talk to each other. There are any number of useful exercises that can grow out of students discussing an issue, problem, or text among themselves. These usually involve the assignment to small groups of a clearly defined task to be done for a short, specified time period.

To start off, the groups should comprise only two or three individuals in order to get almost everyone involved. In general, groups of three are more likely to stay on task than are pairs. In larger groups it is easier to opt out and stay silent. After this initial discussion and the preparation of a response or statement by the group, the instructor can call for the responses, or can ask each group to join two or three other groups to exchange, compare, and summarize responses. How large these can get will depend in part on the configuration of the room in which you are teaching. This step can be repeated until groups reach maximum workable size, at which point they report to the whole class. Overheads or the board can be used at this point, as described above for the one-minute exercises.

Another way to configure this same exercise is to do it twice, first at the beginning of the class where pairs or triads of students give each other their initial take on an issue or subject. Then after a lecture on the subject you can have the same groups revisit the issue and compare responses with their preliminary conclusions. These responses do not always have to be communicated to the whole class.

Team Teaching

One of the most effective ways to keep a large class lively and to introduce variety in instruction is to use more than one instructor in a course. I find that I benefit from team teaching as much as my students do, since the interaction with a colleague energizes me and gets me thinking in new ways, as well as relieving me of some of the burden of teaching and being responsible for so many students. Typically, however, such courses use what I describe below as the tag-team approach and are merely serially taught by two or more instructors.

Other, more interactive or interdependent strategies are available, however, and can allow for much more variety and even excitement for both instructors and students. In some of its forms, team teaching can involve interaction at the front of the class, and that alone can encourage students to participate more, especially when they see and understand that there is more than one way of practising and interpreting the discipline. There is a possible downside to this, in that too much divergence in opinion or approach can confuse students, especially at an introductory level. Hence team teaching style has to be adapted to the particular course and topic. At its best, however, team teaching has provided some of the most memorable, exciting, and satisfying classroom experiences that I and my students have had.

The tag team

This is the most common form of team teaching, where two or more instructors and teaching assistants divide up the course material and take turns lecturing. It works well enough, provides some variety, and plays to the strengths of the various instructors. It is most effective when all instructors attend all classes so that course material can be kept inter-related, or when one course coordinator does the lion's share of the teaching and holds the course together (see *The specialists* below). All instructors should be involved in deciding on the type of student assessment to be used (tests, exams, assignments), both for the course as a whole and the individual components.

The specialists

This is also a common form of team teaching, where a course coordinator is the one constant in a section, and specialists are brought in to teach discrete units or for single lectures.

This method can work well too, especially if the coordinator is careful to let the specialists know:

- what is happening generally in the course, in terms of both content and methodology;
- at what level the specialist's contribution should be pitched;
- what is happening in the course immediately before and after the specialist's class(es)

Such specialists should also be involved in devising the assessment tasks for the section they have taught.

The dance: You lead, I'll follow

This is a method that involves fluid interaction between two instructors, and requires mutual comfort, trust, and respect. Here two instructors with common expertise undertake to teach a class together. One is charged with the main responsibility for the lecture, and outlines and introduces the topics according to a predetermined plan. The other instructor adds supplementary material as appropriate.

The rehearsed improvisation

This is a variant on the dance. The two instructors together develop an outline of the class, setting out its topics and the time for each, generally figuring out the line of argument through the lecture. Instructors can take the lead for various parts of the class, but that does not have to be predetermined. Generally both instructors are prepared on all of the topics, and the lecture flows back and forth between them extemporaneously. Many instructors teach best when there is a degree of danger involved: this method allows for that, but with the safety net of the other lecturer ready to leap to the rescue.

The debate or panel discussion

Two or more instructors pick positions or sides on an issue or problem, and formally present those positions to the class while attempting to refute the other side(s). Teaching assistants and even students can get involved in this. The approach seems to work best when students are invited to join the discussion after its formal elements have been concluded.

The animator and recorder

There are many types of interactive exercise that benefit from having student responses recorded on the board or overhead for later use, or as a way of confirming the value of those responses. I have mentioned different interactive strategies in the previous section. Team teaching allows one instructor to lead the discussion, recognize and respond to contributors, while the other acts as recorder and summarizer. The recorder is not only modelling for students what record of the discussion they might be keeping, he or she is also indicating that students can learn things of value from their fellow students. The recorder can often group responses so as to help students see connections among parts of the topic being discussed. An experienced recorder is also in a better position than the animator to do a useful summary of the discussion and highlight its most important points. Alternatively, the two instructors could do the debriefing together.

The high wire act

This is just what it sounds like, and should only be attempted by those who thrive on danger in the classroom, who know their subject for the day really well, and for people who are really comfortable working together. This is a version of "You lead, I'll follow," but without the "You lead," Instead, one might say, "I'll start and we'll see what happens."

Outside The Lecture Hall

Tutorials and teaching assistants

Perhaps the best way to compensate for the more or less insidious effects of very large lecture sections is through the provision of weekly or bi-weekly small group tutorials. This is a common strategy in many departments, especially those with graduate programs, but it is a strategy far too often begun with little initial thought or later supervision. Because tutorials can have so many obvious benefits, and are in fact small, we seem to believe that merely instituting and holding them will reap every possible benefit, as if there were nothing between wilderness and harvest but throwing a few seeds around.

All too often the utility of a tutorial will depend on the instincts or talent of a first-time teacher whose preparation for the task may have been no more than attendance at a teaching-assistant training day. And just as is the case for faculty, perhaps even more so, these teaching assistants have often earned their positions by being good at solitary rather than public or interpersonal things. They got into graduate school almost exclusively on the basis of grades. Some will no doubt be brilliant teachers, some will be merely ineffectual, and others may actually harm their students. Rather than rehearsing a catalogue of woes here, I am going to list and discuss briefly a number of suggestions that can help make the most of tutorials and tutorial leaders. The actual conduct of tutorials is material for another handbook. Here we are more concerned with the care and feeding of teaching assistants, and with administrative matters concerning tutorials.

The make-up of tutorials

They seem to work best for groups of five or six, but I have seen them function satisfactorily for up to 20 students, especially if you can break that number down to sub-groups of five or six for particular exercises. My experience suggests that if the goal is to encourage active or participatory learning, it is better to have smaller groups meet once every two weeks than to have larger groups meet every week.

Tutorials and seminars also work best when they have stable membership, when they are regularly scheduled classes rather then drop-in-at-your-need-or-convenience sessions. In my own large courses, I assign attendance (and participation) marks for tutorials, but not for lectures. I tell students regularly, not just once at the beginning of the year, that the tutorials are the most important part of the course, and I explain why this is so. If you can only have optional tutorials or drop-in centres, attendance will improve if each week you announce specific topics or problems that will be discussed in those sessions.

Working with teaching assistants or tutorial leaders

Although your first responsibilities are to your subject and your students, and it is you that must take final responsibility for what happens in your section, your teaching assistants naturally accept and share those responsibilities. A cooperative approach to managing and running the course is best, although this does not mean that you can or should load administrative or other responsibilities on to graduate teaching assistants unless they have been specifically engaged to perform those duties. Indeed, you owe it your TAs and their future careers to remind them to manage their limited time carefully, to not let the very immediate demands and rewards of teaching threaten or steal time from other important aspects of their graduate student careers.

You should provide explicit and full instructions to your teaching assistants on the way you want them to conduct tutorials and manage their students. It is a good idea to prepare a detailed list of TAs' duties in the course, including the amount of time you expect them to spend on various functions. This can even be done as a sort of contract that is signed by both parties. Beyond that, think carefully not just about things like the management and marking of assignments and tests, but also about the sort of style you want to use in tutorials, the degree of formality or informality you would like to encourage. Do this in special sessions before the beginning of the term, and regularly throughout the course. I usually meet with my teaching assistants weekly.

Weekly course meetings

I like to plan the week's tutorials cooperatively, and to discuss particular exercises we might use. While I encourage variety and a degree of experimentation by my TAs, sometimes we will all do the same thing in the same way. For instance, we might all closely examine an assigned passage from a text by giving individual students responsibility for discussing a few lines of the passage, and then go over the relevant chapter in the composition text. For other tutorials we might all discuss the same text, theme, or problem in our own ways, and at our meeting we would discuss a number of strategies that seem appropriate.

We also use meetings to plan and discuss future assignments. I try to involve tutorial leaders in setting assignments and tests, although there are a few things to be wary of. The first is that we must always be careful not to exploit TAs by making unfair demands of their time. Consequently, I always make such contributions voluntary: I ask for suggestions for questions or other exercises. And while I ask my teaching assistants to look over essay and other assignments before I give them to the class, I do not show them beforehand copies of tests or exams that will be given to the whole class. This is not because I do not trust them, but because it gives them a freer hand in helping students to prepare for such tests.

In these meetings we work together at achieving marking parity. This may not be a problem if you take the common route of using only machine-scorable evaluation instruments, but it is different if you use either short-answer or essay-type assignments. I teach large sections of courses where the essay remains the dominant means of evaluation, a luxury made possible by having TAs (and — much more rarely — markers). After every assignment is submitted, we meet to go over the marking of that assignment and try as much as possible to establish a standard, using the following steps:

- I select some sample answers to the current assignment (usually four or five). This can be done randomly, but I prefer to ensure some variety in mark ranges.
- I make enough photocopies of the sample assignment in advance so that all the TAs can look at it as I read it aloud. One copy for every two or three TAs is enough, and these should be collected and recycled at the end of the session: it is unfair to students to circulate unauthorized copies of their papers.
- After we have gone through the assignment (or exam answer) aloud, each TA and I privately assign it a mark.
- We then go around the table, with each person announcing the assigned mark and the reasons for that particular mark. Sometimes, especially after the first paper, a quick round of just announcing marks or letter grades is followed by asking why the persons who assigned the most extreme marks did so. For the first assignment or question, I will often only ask for a mark range: Is this an A, B, C, D, or F? Why? After the discussion, I will explain what mark I would like to see that assignment receive, and why. My mark may not be any more accurate an assessment of the worth of that assignment than anybody else's, but in the end I must take responsibility and establish standards for my section. In my experience, after as few as three and rarely more than five assignments, my TAs will be assigning marks within 3-4% of one another, which is good enough for me.
- We carry through this procedure for every assignment. You cannot just do this in a workshop on marking at the beginning of the year and then forget about it.
- The same TAs regularly mark the same section of the class, so that students know who to talk to about assignments and grades.
- There are dangers associated with this process too. Unless the instructor in charge of the section is very vigilant, regularly samples marked papers, and encourages markers to use the range of marks available, the range itself tends to be compressed.

Weekly course meetings are also the time to bring up any problems or conspicuous successes we are having in tutorials. These could include problems with student conduct or participation in tutorials, although I discourage the citing of individual student names. This is also the time to talk about successful or unsuccessful teaching strategies we have used. Use the TAs as sounding boards to learn the problems students have with lecture materials. Then you can know what you have to go over again in lectures or do differently next year, and even what texts or other parts of the course might need change. For these reasons and others, I always take a tutorial group myself, so that I have a more direct way to gauge with a small group how successfully the large classes are running.

We also use these meetings to arrange for people to cover for one another as inevitably will be necessary with a group of committed and busy people. I find it is better to make these arrangements when we are all together than to leave responsibility to the individual TA. This is part of encouraging all of us to understand that the class is a cooperative venture that involves us all.

Support for TAs

Students are generally quick to interpret power structures, and unless they understand correctly the role and importance of teaching assistants, they will often challenge their authority, or attempt to circumvent the TA and deal directly with the course instructor. It is important that you publicly establish your TA's role and status right at the beginning of the course. You should also make clear what procedures students are to follow in getting help on assignments, or in those instances where they are unhappy or puzzled about a particular mark on an essay or exam.

Another strategy to reinforce TA credibility is to have them give parts of lectures, especially early in the year, to the big class. You can also call on TAs when you are stumped by a student question, or are groping to remember something, using them as a sort of knowledge bank or brains trust. When you look to the TAs for such help, the class picks up cues from your manifest respect for them.

If you have a large number of teaching assistants, it is useful to hold one or more special office hours a week (separate from your normal office hours for seeing undergraduates) when they can come to consult you. At least once a year, and preferably once each term, sit in on a tutorial conducted by each of your teaching assistants, and follow that up with a discussion of what went well and what might have gone better. Be gentle! These visits will also help you a great deal in composing references or letters for your teaching assistants' dossiers.

Evaluation

Evaluation is another subject that requires a handbook of its own, and on which a great deal has been written. Typically, most evaluation in large classes is done by machine-scorable, multiple-choice tests. While it is true that a well-devised set of such questions can test a great deal more than knowledge recognition, there are still many educational objectives we want students to meet that are not tested by such instruments.

There should always be a good match between the knowledge and skills you expect students to gain in your course and the evaluation instruments you use. You may have to convince your department chair to provide you with marking money or enough teaching assistants to carry out evaluation appropriately. Large classes are put in place to save money, but that does not mean that they should be run as cheaply as possible. The same goes for use of teaching aids, which is the subject of the next section.

Teaching Aids And Technology:
The Well-equipped Classroom

In every large classroom the equipment listed below should be mounted so that the instructor can control it from a lockable console at the front of the room. Control can either be direct or via remote controls, as in the case of slide projectors. The lighting in the room should also be controllable from the front, and the lighting mix should include dimmable incandescent lights. Fluorescent lights flicker horribly when they are dimmed, and students protest vigorously. Remote controls for the equipment (always desirable), the computer keyboard (where available), the laser pointer, and the wireless microphones (with fresh spare batteries and spare clips) should be stored in a lockable drawer in the console. Here are three lists of desirable equipment for classes of different sizes.

For classes between 50-125:

Chalkboards. If you are using the boards for more than writing down the odd term or name, and even then, experiment before classes. Check what you can see from various angles and distances. You may find that only the centre part of the board array is usable, and that you have to write much larger than usual. If you can find it, there is oversize chalk.

At least one projection screen, preferably two.

At least one overhead projector.

A video/data projector.

A laserdisk/CD player.

An audiocassette deck or DAT (digital audio) deck.

A VCR.

A wireless microphone if the class reaches the upper end of this range.

A good sound system.

In most cases you will have to import a *slide projector* because it is a little awkward to store, but the room should allow you to install it easily and it should be controllable from the front console.

For classes of 125-400:

Two bright overhead projectors.

Two screens, one angled at a front corner of the room, the other centrally located and wide enough to accommodate the images from two overhead projectors.

A video/data projector. A rear projection screen for this projector and for slides is highly desirable because this enables you to show images quite clearly without turning off the room lights.

A laserdisk/CD (often called a multidisk) player. This should be programmable, and allow for chapter and other searches.

A Videocassette Player.

An audiocassette and/or DAT deck.

A built-in computer with a long keyboard cable to enable instructors to use presentation programs and other computer-generated images, and with an *internet hookup.*

A slide projector should be easily available and installable. The room and its remote systems should allow for those disciplines that will want to use two slide projectors, either side by side or with a cross-fader.

A laser pointer.

Two wireless microphones.

A very good sound system.

For classes of 400+:

As for classes of 125-400, but:

The video/data projector has to be superbright (much more costly than projectors usually found in classrooms), and rear projection is even more desirable.

Even a bright overhead projector may not be enough. There are apparatuses called visual presenters available through educational technology providers. These project overhead-type images through your video-data projector.

The sound system has to be excellent.

A smoke machine and a set of assorted mirrors. Just kidding, but there will be days when you feel that you need these. Teaching classes this size is a performance art.

A Few Parting But Not Final Words

After 25 years of teaching large classes, I still feel that I have a lot to learn about them, and I continue to learn new ways of doing things from the literature in the field, from my talented colleagues across the country who have shared their ideas with me, and from the students who kindly put up with my experiments in the classroom. Although some aspects of teaching large classes are discipline-specific, many techniques and strategies are broadly transferable or adaptable. I hope that you will have found that to be the case with much that is in this handbook.

Among the things that I know apply to all effective teaching of large classes are these. That classes work better when you show your students that you care about them and want them to learn. That you care about and are still deeply interested in, excited about, and moved by the material you are discussing. And that you are still open to new ideas and are still learning.

I also know what happens all too frequently, and does not work, which is to try to terrify first-year students in large classes with the difficulty of what lies ahead of them. One version of this is the old chestnut that enjoins students to look to the left and look to the right while you tell them that one of them will not be back next year. Most of your students are smart people, they deserve to be in university, and we should not resent them because there are so many of them. Do not punish your students for the faults of societies and governments that pay lip service to the high value of education but do not put their money where their mouths are.

Remember that we teach by the model we provide, by the example we give of how we engage with our disciplines. We also teach things about how people relate to each other, so that we must also teach ethically, sensitively, and humanely.

References

Goranson, R. E. (1976). A paradox in educational communication. In I Kusyszn (Ed.), *Teaching and learning process seminars*, Vol. 1. Toronto: York University.

Habeshaw, S., Gibbs G., & Habeshaw, T. (1993). *53 problems with large classes: Making the best of a bad job.* Bristol, England: Technical and Education Services.

Rasmussen, R. V. (1984). Practical discussion techniques for instructors. *AACE Journal, 12* (2), 1984, 38-47.

Weaver, R. L., & Cotrell, H. (1987). Lecturing: Essential communication strategies. In M. G. Weimer (Ed.), *Teaching large classes well* (pp. 57-69). San Francisco: Jossey-Bass.

Suggestions For Further Reading

The following sources are ones I have found especially useful, but many of them may be out of print or otherwise hard to obtain. If your institution has an instructional development centre you will probably find they have a small library of books on teaching and learning in higher education, including materials on teaching large classes. Another useful source of information on large classes is the "Teaching more students" series of short guides, originally developed in England by Graham Gibbs and his colleagues at the Oxford Centre for Staff Development. Six of these guides have been adapted for Canadian use by the Queen's University Instructional Development Centre. Titles available include *Problems and strategies, Lecturing with more students, Discussion with more students, Assessing more students, Independent learning with more students,* and *Course design for more students.*

Andresen, L. W. (1988). *Lecturing to large groups: A guide to doing it less but better* (2nd ed.). Sydney, Australia: University of New South Wales, Professional Development Centre.

Bain, R. K. (1966). On making it play in Peoria. In R. McGee (Ed.), *Teaching the mass class.* Washington, DC: American Sociological Association.

Bowman, J. S. (1979). The lecture-discussion format revisited. *Improving College and University Teaching, 27*(1), 25-27.

Brock, S. C. (1976). *Practitioners' views on teaching the large introductory college course.* Manhattan, KS: Kansas State University, Center for Faculty Evaluation and Development, 1976.

Brooks, D. W. (1984). Alternatives to traditional lecturing. *Journal of Chemical Education, 61,* 858-859.

Coleman, H. (1989). *Learning and teaching in large classes: A bibliography.* Leeds and Lancaster, England: Leeds University, Overseas Education Unit and Lancaster University Department of Linguistics and Modern English.

Cryer, P., & Elton, L. (1992). *Promoting active learning in large classes.* Sheffield, England: Sheffield Universities Staff Development and Training Unit.

Frederick, J. (1987). Student involvement: Active learning in large classes. In M. G. Weimer (Ed.), *Teaching large classes well* (pp. 45-56). San Francisco: Jossey-Bass.

Gibbs, G., Habeshaw, S., & Habeshaw, T. (1992). *53 interesting ways to teach large classes.* Bristol, England: Technical and Educational Services.

Gibbs, G., & Jenkins, A. (Eds.). (1992). *Teaching large classes in higher education.* London: Kogan Page.

Gleason. M. (1986). Better communication in large courses. *College Teaching, 34*(1), 20-24.

Kain, E. (1986). The mass class as theatre: Suggestions for improving the chances of a hit production. In R. McGee (Ed.), *Teaching the mass class* (pp. 85-98). Washington, DC: American Sociological Association.

Magin, D., Nightingale, P., Andresen, L., & Boud, D. (1993). *Strategies for increasing students' independence.* Kensington, Australia: University of New South Wales, Professional Development Centre.

McGee, R. (1991). *Handling hordes: Teaching large classes.* West Lafayette, IN: Purdue University, Continuing Education Office.

McGee, R. (Ed.). (1996). *Teaching the mass class.* Washington, DC: American Sociological Association.

McKeachie, W. J. (1994). *Teaching tips: A guidebook for the beginning college teacher* (10th ed.). Lexington, MA: Heath.

Michaelson, L. K. (1983). Team learning in large classes. In C. Bouton & R. Y. Garth (Eds.), *Learning in groups.* San Francisco: Jossey-Bass.

Monk, G. S. (1983). Student engagement and teacher power in large classes. In C. Bouton & R. Y. Garth (Eds.), *Learning in groups* . San Francisco: Jossey-Bass,

Teaching Large Classes. (n.d.). Urbana-Champaign, IL: University of Illinois, Office of Instructional and Management Services.

Weaver, R. L. (1983). The small group in large classes. *Educational Forum, 48*(1), 65-73.

Weimer, M. G. (Ed.). (1987). *Teaching large classes well.* San Francisco: Jossey-Bass.

Wolford, G. L., & Smith, W. H. (Eds.). (1975). *Large course instruction. Hanover, NH: Dartmouth College, Office of Instructional Services and Educational Psychology.*

STLHE Membership

If you are interested in a forum for the exchange of ideas and information on post-secondary teaching and learning; if you believe that teaching is important and that dedication to its improvement should be recognized; if you feel that the road to professional improvement is best walked in the company of enthusiastic peers; then you should join the Society.

Membership is open to anyone who supports the aims of the Society. Information on individual and institutional memberships can be obtained from the Society.

Julia Christensen Hughes (jchriste@uoguelph.ca)
c/o Teaching Support Services
University of Guelph
Guelph, Ontario   N1G 2W1
www.stlhe.ca

Ordering Green Guides
To order please contact

The Book Store at Western
University Community Centre
The University of Western Ontario
London, Ontario   N6A 3K7
Phone: (519) 661-3520
Fax: (519) 661-3673
E-mail: bkstor@uwo.ca
Web: www.bookstore.uwo.ca